Free Verses for Young Readers

Talented Poet at lulu.com

ISBN: 978-1-257-00766-0

This is a collection of the most popular poems written by Jingle during 2010, free style and very profound rhyming.

Both adults and young kids will find joy and laughter in this collection, make sure read aloud when you come cross poems on dogs, cats, super bowl games…

Special Thanks to my family members and online writing communities for the encouragement and inspirations…I won't be where I am without your support.

Jingle, Feb 15, 2011

Free Verses for Young Readers

No Nosy Naughty Noises

Nap now in serenity,

No New York Times news,

No nosy naughty noises.

The Smell of Life

The smell of life

floats somewhere,

as if stars were dragon's breath

and they were breathed on earth.

Daddy is researching on life's birth.

Three lovely kids joined him to guess.

They behave like a thinking tank,

digging deep about life's many a prank.

They recall

times when they throw the ball

until it's too dark to see it at all,

And the smell of life starts to fall

As if a dragon breathed

on them, prime time.

Fun is earthed,

Blinking their eyes,

Four silly bunnies sniff their noses

and they have the best appetites

for life, because

life could smell like roses.

I Read, I Live!

As a child,

My imagination often runs wild,

I would close my eyes

To shut off ghosts lurking near my bed,

I would roll a dice

if fears start to dominate my head.

I read many graphic novels,

I watched many classical films,

I have juggled marbles,

I listened to folktales in big volumes.

Dreams in the red chamber may be fancy,

Witches in horror movies may be sneaky,

But a fiction is a fiction,

Fictions evoke thrill to evoke addiction.

With each clash,

Upon every crash,

Children's world is enriched in a flash,

Writers are definitely making big flash

by letting the creative fire burn to ash.

As a child,

My imagination often runs wild.

I read,

I live,

I grow,

I achieve.

I write,

I share,

and care!

Hope

Too small for U. S. Cents,

Too rare to be in historical museum,

Too heavy to make sense,

Too abstract to dwell in hands of a child,

.

A shooting star soars cross the sky,

A spark flashes through squeezing rocks,

A lightening flies by,

A basket of wool to make warm socks,

.

All promises freeze like ice,

All greetings ring like bells.

All gamblers focus on the dice,

All smiles ripple under the spells.

.

Hides behind the time that flies,

Dance in the hands that knit ties.

Hope is like the invisible air,

It makes stirs everywhere….

Juvenile Judgment Is No Fun!

Juvenile judgment is no fun,

Be the just, judicious, and respectful one,

and jump 4 bliss, done!

I Is 4 I

I die

4 apple pie,

I cry

2 have a try,

I sigh

and aim high,

I fly

in the sky.

I am I

Who can be shy,

I buy

a tie,

I glide

with pride,

I inspire

and never expire!

I approve

and improve,

I survive

and

thrive…

And The Fun Never Ends

A baby Fairy dragon is very merry
For he's going fishing with Dad Terry,
Up and down,
He dances around
In his cheery little town
Until he sees what he stumbles upon:
Standing in front of him
Is a violet flower
That looks sad and slim
And holds No power,
"What's going on?"
The green dragon asks with a frown.
"Although full of grace,

Stuck in one single place,

No freedom to explore

the world like others do,

how can my dreams come true?"

The young flower is in tears

holding all those sadness and fears.

The fairy understands her blues.

This is something she can never choose.

He turns on his magical power

and grants the wishes of the poor flower:

They have made an adventurous escape

and recorded everything in a video tape.

The flower has gone fishing with her new friends,

And the fun never ends.

I Imagine We Do Space Dance

It's a lovely summer morning,

I am in my room, sitting.

I let my window open,

I breathes fresh air

While waiting for something to happen,

I see a bird in despair.

It's a baby bird,

It looks rather sad.

I want to invite it in,

Yet I have no idea how to begin.

It hurts

that this cutie is away from its parents.

I don't want to scare it away,

Thus I stay put
Daring not to say
anything, bad or good.
Recalling my mom's kiss
On my cheeks,
I reckon this bird must miss
its mom for weeks.
I want to have a chance
To play with it in the wild,
I imagine we do space dance
To entertain the world.
"what have you found?"
I feel the lips
And hear the words,
As I turn around,

I see toy ships

And game swords.

Oh, my,

I give a heavy sign,

The bird is disturbed and is gone,

I ask my mom to leave me alone!

Curiosity Drives Us Nuts

Curiosity drives us nuts,

Ignoring parents' no buts,

We run to the woods

To spicy up our moods,

What we see

has made our day!

160 fairies r at play

on Sunday!

Did You Know?

Did you know?
Did you know
kids in your neighborhood's lives?
Did your friends show
their fears, struggles, or how horrified to
see men ignore their wives?
It is hard to tell
In general.
But hearing a scream from next door,
My brother and I jump out of our chairs
and hold our breath on the floor,
Is their house on fire?
they have a fight for unfulfilled desire?

As kids,

We don't understand many things,

A family life could be romantic,

It could also be problematic!

We wonder why parents love to complain

as their marriages are entitled to remain?

We hope that nothing bad happens,

Patiently, we will wait for our parents.

…

Between You and Me

When I don't know U,

And U don't know me,

I dreamed of getting to know somebody,

That somebody could be anyone,

including U.

.

When U don't know me,

And I don't know U,

I pictured in my head for my dreams to

come true,

Upon then, life will be upgraded,

fresh and anew.

.

Between U and me,

There are distances, near or far,

Between U and me,

There are roadblocks keeping us apart.

.

The journey connecting U and me

could be invisible,

The light that guides you to me

could be magical,

.

Does the road wind all the way uphill?

Maybe yes, maybe no,

If yes,

do we have to continue with strong will?

Of course, I believe so.

.

We meet via the words written in books,

Or with the click of a mouse,

Joy and satisfaction surface

regardless one's looks,

As we network

without leaving the house.

Beach Is A Great Place To Explore

My name is Pitten.

My age is seven.

I love collecting seashells on the shore,

I enjoy playing the sand and more.

Beach is a great place to explore,

Beach time has improved my arithmetic score.

I know how to add, subtract, and even multiply,

It is as easy as an apply pie.

1 times 7 is 7,

Add 4 years I turn eleven.

2 times 7 is 14,

That's when I become a real teen.

3 times 7 is 21,

I love watching the rising sun.

4 times 7 is 28,

Doing math unit is simply great.

5 times 7 is 35,

I enjoy leaning how to dive.

6 times 7 is 42,

I choose an ocean over a pool.

7 times 7 is 49,

Running barefoot is so much fun.

8 times 7 is 56,

Life is full of numerical tricks.

9 times 7 is 63,

Swimming near a beach makes me feel

FREE.

. . .

My name is Pitten,

My age is 7,

I love collecting seashells on the shore,

I enjoy playing the sand and more.

Beach is a great place to explore,

Beach time has improved my arithmetic score…

The Ring of The Phone

Just like the ripples of water
When throwing in a stone,
The rings of the phone
make stirring sound.
Lan's heart beats
furiously
As she gives her puppy some treats
Nervously.
The phone keeps ringing,
"Woof, woof,"
Boots barks, waiting,
Lan scoops her up,
"Hello, what's up?"

"..."

What does she hear?

U tell me, dear!

A New Baby Is Born

A new baby is born,
Full of freshness and light;
Promising future to be held,
Everything will be alright.
Remaining a curious mind
in his pilgrimage,
By the blessings of angels' heart;
Humble and daring,
He is to blaze the trail
in the honor of God.
Smile now,
Grow strong and tall;
No need to wonder how,

Simply live to give love 2 all.

Name him Bingle,

Make him giggle

And wiggle,

Enjoy the magical moments,

wink and twinkle!

Life Goes On

Tissue by tissue to a soul one grows,
As leaf by leaf the trees become trees,
Day by day, one learns and sows,
when the sun has fun seeing breeze.
.....
Seeds of hope give one wings to fly,
One either winnowed to earth
Or whirled to the sky.
Life goes on,
Some survive while others die.
.....
Wrinkles of a splash, on the water cease,
Body and soul,

bend and stretch like these.

Elements to elements, cells to cells,

Individuals to individuals,

dream for peace.

.....

Feel the coolness when cool winds blow,

Listen to the music

when the lure vibrates with its bow.

Giggle baby alike

while enjoy the nature's show,

Mark down your innocence

when the days are covered with snow.

A Squirrel Flirts With A Nut

Tickled by dancing breeze,
A squirrel flirts with a nut
while sitting bolt upright below the trees.

Verses on a Farm

Open your eyes,

Be nice,

Don't forget to say goodbyes.

A sheep

Is asleep

in a moving jeep.

A pig may be fat,

A pig may be lazy,

A pig may be a friend to a cat named Daisy.

A wild duck

In the park

Dreams about GOOD luck.

A wise hen

Teaches her chicken

how to count from one to ten.

A true friend

Is someone who does amend

and cares for **YOU** from start to end.

A Blue Fish Is Ready 2 Play

Deep in the sea,
On a sunny day,
A blue fish is ready to play.

To her dismay,
A shark is coming her way,
The blue fish could become a prey.

Detecting the shark in her harm's way,
The blue fish sums up her bravery,
and invites the shark to party next day.

The shark winked to agree,

The blue fish is free

on her way to her favorite bay.

It is another beautiful day,

With the shark guarding the doorway,

a school of fish have fish cake 4 the day!

Poetry on Spring

Colors
And Rains
Are what spring brings.

Spring
Is when
The fun and life begin.

Doors open
The air is fresh,
fountains splash.

It is spring time,

Farms plow,

Trees sprout.

I would like

Ride a bike

And go on a hike.

Sing

About spring

in a fling.

Snow and ice melt

Buckle your seat belt

Drive with NO guilt.

Schools keep open,

Hens are ready to hatch chicken,

Blossoms wave hello in the garden.

4 Amy

Amy is the water in dry desert,

The air on earth,

and the pink roses on Valentine's day.

Amy's place

Is full of grace

and shines to embrace.

Amy and her family

are the treasure

of beauty and pleasure.

Amy is the one

Who projects FUN
under the sun.

Amy loves U,
For being true
and for what U do!

Amy's friendship
Is precious
and delicious.

Poems on Summer

Do a somersault
With no fault
on a Somerset.

Pass summer nights
With tales about pirates
and stories about fairies.

Do a bunk
To get ride of Stinky
Skunk.

Toss a dime

Make something rhythm
For Summer time.

Birds stretch their wings
to sail above the mountains
And seek drinking fountains.

Put on sun-block lotion,
Have your slippers on motion
before go deep in the ocean.

I can not see
In the sea
When I get seasick!

Not to wink
at the sink
That starts to look pink.

A sparrow
shall not swallow
any arrow.

The Mountain awakes
As snow melts
And water floods the lakes.

Bake me a pie,
Stay by my side,
Fly my favorite kite.

I cannot wait

For the summer heat

to quit.

The day is hot,

Your attitude is cool,

Let's have a feast of Haiku.

Your voice vibrates,

Your eyes sparkle

like diamonds.

Never attend

Summer camps

Near muddy swamps.

Dream summer dreams,
Beam summer beams,
Swim summer swims.

Breathe summer air,
Reduce summer despair,
Play summer games fair.

Walk summer walks,
Talk summer talks,
Paint summer on your sidewalks.

Facing a beehive,

One shall dive

to survive.

A seashell

And a door bell

Get along well.

When hot and cold air clashes,

Thunders roll,

lightening flashes.

The Sun

Has fun

Painting you tan.

I wish I may,

I wish I might,

I wish for a pool to swim in tonight.

Like fire,

The sun bakes

while you hunger for snow-cakes.

A swimming pool

Is a tool

to stay cool.

A lightning bug is a firefly

Who winks at a butterfly

and teases at a dragonfly.

I eat a peach
Before I teach
at a beach.

The sky is blue,
The clouds are white,
The sun screams with burning sunlight.

When the day is hot,
Fish go hide under water
in the deepest spot.

Summer is tall
In comparison
with Spring and Fall.

Verses on Super Bowl

Super bowl game
is a F-O-O-T-B-A-L-L game
With F-O-O-T barely on the ball most of
the time in game.

A show
will be on
before the game is on.

An alien can not tell
the difference between a soccer ball
and a football.

Soccer players kick the ball,

Football players throw the ball,

Both players run and pass the ball.

A Super bowl game

is a foot-ball game

Not a food-bowl game.

Play the game fair,

Play the game fun,

Celebrate the game with a bottle of wine.

Super bowl fans are here,

Super bowl fans are there,

Super bowl fans are everywhere.

Sit still,

Swallow a pill,

Stay alert about fire drill.

Cheers,

Tears,

music in ears.

Cameras,

Lights,

sparkling eyes.

Super bowl tickets for sale,

Not restricted to a male,

one dollar a pail.

Did U C

What I C? (did you see what I see?)

The ball is flying your way.

1 2, buckle my shoe,

3, 4, sit on the floor,

5, 6, bake super bowl cakes.

Go,

Catch my favorite ball,

Steal today's show.

It hurts

When one loses

and Walk like gooses.

Walk super bowl walk,

Talk super bowl talks,

Paint super bowl trophy on sidewalks.

Super bowl is hot,

Super bowl fans are cool,

Let's have a feast of super bowl Haiku.

Super bowl game is wholesome,

Super bowl players are winsome,

Super bowl fans and are handsome.

A football

And a super bowl'

Are twins in the show.

Verses on Cats:

Feeling alone,

Kittens meow at a microphone

to sing a song.

Cats on mat,

Cats in hat,

Cats hunger for a pat.

Please don't be sad

Or mad

at your cat.

A cat

Wants to hurt

A rat.

Running up the hill

Is the kitty Jill

Who barely stay still.

Some cats are black,

Some cats are white,

All cats are bright.

My name is Pat,

I am a special cat

who enjoys wearing a hat.

I am a kitten

Who is willing to listen

And eat fish often.

2010 little mittens

Fit

1005 cute kittens.

A kitten

Hides a mitten

in kitchen.

A rat

Sneaks a tit for tat

to challenge a cat!

Feeling cozy,

I curled like a ball

and napped against the wall.

A cat

Named Pat

swings a baseball bat.

My fur is silky,

My voice is milky,

My jaws are poky.

That fat

Cat

is my Dad.

Stay put,

Be in mood,

Enjoy cat food.

Verses on Dogs

Dogs enjoy
Playing a toy
with a boy.

You throw,
I catch,
We are a perfect match.

If stuck,
Ducks quack,
Dogs bark.

Dogs are in good

Mood

in protecting your neighborhood.

When the boatmen fail

To sail,

Dogs wail.

I bark

In the dark

at *Mark*.

I dressed up as a big

Pig

Wearing a wig.

From head

To toe,

I carry No odd smell.

Hairy,

Merry,

I make a friend with *Sherry*.

Dogs can be big,

Dogs can be small,

Dogs can take vacations at a shopping mall.

That chubby

Puppy

is happy.

I am a dog
Who can doggy walk
on sidewalk.

Home alone,
I answer the phone
with my barking sound.

As a hunter,
The dog stalks the woods
with wonder.
If you are new,
I will bark at you
and bite your shoe.

When a gift comes in mail,

The dog will not wail,

But wiggles his tail!

What do you think?

Verses on Snow Storms

It is not nice

For Santa to sacrifice

Because of stormy ice!

Get warm,

Get warm,

Santa appreciates No ice-storm!

You scream,

I scream,

We all scream to stop ice storm.

Like it or not,

Harry Potter is a wizard,
I am a blizzard.

When ice dreams
About ice creams,
Ice beams.

Snow worms
Play snowball fights
after snow-storms.

Life is a stage,
Put on the show,
Stop the snow.

Icy Bears
Icy Hares
make icy pairs.

Snow snows
Snow souls, and
Snow tells snow tales!

Bright,
White,
I touch your life with pride!

Being in the Divine's good graces,
I descend to earth
To decorate your places!

Lighter than rain,

More popular than frost,

I float in your sight, No cost!

Snow glows,

Snow blows,

Snow steals the shows.

Let it snow,

Let the seeds you sow

Begin to grow!

Snow dances

Space dances

Despite the snow trouble in Finances!

A rectangle is cute,

A square is cuter,

A circle is the cutest.

Cute, Cuter, the Cutest!

A cow is cute,

A cow that gives milk is cuter,

A cow giving quality milk is the cutest.

A cello is cute,

A cello that is played by a boy is cuter,

A cello that is played by a boy to make

the sickly heal is the cutest.

A pumpkin is cute,

A pumpkin with a happy face is cuter,

A pumpkin with a happy face glowing

in the dark is the cutest.

A panda is cute,

A panda in a child's arms is cuter,

A panda in a happy child's arms

is the cutest.

A poem is cute,

A poem that tickles is cuter,

A poem that tickles and inspires

is the cutest.

Bring Home The Best:

Lullaby,

Boys and girls,

Go to sleep,

Dream about aliens and fairies,

Wake up in a flying spaceship.

Lullaby,

Let the world fight,

Let the enemy fall,

Let your ideas of wars offer insight,

Keep standing up tall.

Lullaby,

Dream on and on,

Fly toward the moon,

Leave behind the warnings on the phone,

Come home soon.

Lullaby,

Grownups and children,

Enjoy a good rest,

keep your course sailing in the ocean,

Bring home the best.

What's It?

I have spied something interesting,

all spotty and green,

Behind an elegant lotus leaf,

the thing's eyes are full of mischief,

It hops

to make stops,

what's it?

D Is 4 Delicacy

Delicacy is fancy,

Elegant and choosy,

Lots of softness

in common 2!

a delicious word 2 chew on,

Come along,

Your delicate taste is profound!

Count From 10 to 1, Let Healing Begin

10,9, counting is fun,

8, 7, after ten is eleven,

6, 5, you can survive,

4, 3, reading is free,

2, 1, let it shine.

10, 9, walk and run,

8, 7, odd and even,

6, 5, swimming and dive,

4, 3, oppose and agree,

2, 1, the moon and the sun.

10, 9, draw a line,

8, 7, dream about Heaven,

6, 5, bliss will arrive,

4, 3, plant a tree,

2, 1, everything is fine.

10, 9, hot cross bun,

8, 7, baked in the oven,

6, 5, a fork and a knife,

4, 3, charge No fee,

2, 1, a job well done.

10, 9, praise the Divine,

8, 7, smile often,

6, 5, ready to drive,

4, 3, wait and see,

2, 1, celebrate with wine.

10, 9, I am your fan,

8, 7, my name is Steven,

6, 5, do high five,

4, 3, obtain a degree,

2, 1, let the healing begin.

Count From 10 to 1, Double the Fun!

10-Ten poles, Ten holes;

9-Nine chairs, Nine pears;

8-Eight ducks, Eight trucks;

7-Seven games, Seven names;

6-six dolls, Six rolls;

5-Five hoses, Five noses;

4-Four trains, Four stains;

3-Three chicks, Three tricks;

2-Two jars, Two cars;

1-One computer, One commuter.

10 9 8 7 6 5 4 3 2 1,

Double your holiday fun!

Count from 1 to 10, Smile again!

1, 2, go to the zoo,

3, 4, shop at the store,

5, 6, build with bricks,

7, 8, sugar is sweet.

9, 10, buy me a pen.

1, 2, Winnie the pooh,

3, 4, eat with a paw,

5, 6, search for beehives,

7, 8, honey tastes great,

9, 10, hungry again.

1, 2, an owl says hoot,

3, 4, tigers roar,

5, 6, a fox hides in a box,

7, 8, a bird says tweet,

9, 10, stay in the den.

1, 2, cows say moo,

3, 4, two walls make a hall,

5, 6, chew the grass,

7, 8, breed in high rate,

9, 10, big fat hen.

1, 2, ghosts say boo,

3, 4, stop the snore,

5, 6, do more tricks,

7, 8, juggle one more plate,

9, 10, birds love to sing.

1, 2, swim in a pool,

3, 4, relax on the shore,

5, 6, a baby kicks,

7, 8, hold his feet,

9, 10, vacation comes to an end.

1, 2, back to school,

3, 4, obey the law,

5, 6, solve some problems,

7, 8, never quit,

9, 10, it is fun to learn.

1, 2, sit on a stool,

3, 4, play with a see-saw,

5, 6, enjoy birthday cakes,

7, 8, find a nice classmate,

9, 10, high grades remain.

1, 2, peek-a-boo,

3, 4, open the door,

5, 6, attend some classes,

7, 8, have a good fate,

9, 10, credits regain.

1, 2, take a tool,

3, 4, find a saw,

5, 6, cut the glass,

7, 8, length, width, and height,

9, 10, things to mend.

1, 2, who is who?
3, 4, sweep the floor,
5, 6, wear only socks,
7, 8, take a seat,
9, 10, give her a ring.

1, 2, food to chew,
3, 4, avoid mouth sore,
5, 6, mice love cheese,
7, 8, pies to bake,
9, 10, let the party begin.

1, 2, tie your shoe,

3, 4, open the door,

5, 6, check the mailbox,

7, 8, get in line and wait,

9, 10, finally win.

1, 2, dreams come true,

3, 4, sleep no more,

5, 6, surprises for Christmas,

7, 8, Santa stays up late,

9, 10, sleepy again.

(These are inspired by a counting song, 1 2, buckle my shoe…)

Count from 1 to 10, Once again!

1-One family, One Humanity;

2-Two parents, Two presents;

3-Three boys, Three toys;

4-Four bedrooms, Four bathrooms;

5-Five faces, Five shoelaces;

6-Six cats, Six Rats;

7-Seven crowns, Seven clowns;

8-Eight mops, Eight maps;

9-Nine dishes, Nine wishes;

10-Ten arms, Ten legs!

Count from one to ten, once again!

Let the magic show in numbers begin!

www.ingramcontent.com/pod-product-compliance
Ingram Content Group UK Ltd.
Pitfield, Milton Keynes, MK11 3LW, UK
UKHW040559210726
13854UKWH00008B/1498